## GLOBAL CULTURES

# Chinese Culture

Mary Colson

**www.raintreepublishers.co.uk**
Visit our website to find out
more information about
Raintree books.

**To order:**
☎ Phone 0845 6044371
▤ Fax +44 (0) 1865 312263
✉ Email myorders@raintreepublishers.co.uk

Customers from outside the UK please telephone +44 1865 312262

Raintree is an imprint of Capstone Global
Library Limited, a company incorporated
in England and Wales having its registered
office at 7 Pilgrim Street, London, EC4V
6LB – Registered company number: 6695582

Edited by Charlotte Guillain, Abby Colich,
  and Vaarunika Dharmapala
Designed by Steve Mead
Original illustrations © Capstone Global
  Library Ltd 2013
Illustrations by Oxford Designers & Illustrators
Picture research by Ruth Blair
Originated by Capstone Global Library Ltd
Printed and bound in Singapore

ISBN 978 1 406 24173 0 (hardback)
16 15 14 13 12
10 9 8 7 6 5 4 3 2 1

**British Library Cataloguing in Publication Data**
Colson, Mary.
Chinese culture. -- (Global cultures)
306'.0951-dc23
A full catalogue record for this book is
available from the British Library.

**Acknowledgements**
We would like to thank the following for
permission to reproduce photographs:
Alamy pp. 13 (© The Art Archive), 20 (©
Robert Harding Picture Library Ltd), 25 (©
John Warburton-Lee Photography), 29 (©
dbimages), 31 (© Jon Arnold Images Ltd),
37 (© Photos 12); Corbis pp. 5 (© Gong Lei/
Xinhua Press), 8 (© Royal Ontario Museum),
10 (© Justin Guariglia), 11 (© Peng Zhen Ge/
Redlink), 12 (© Fritz Hoffmann/In Pictures),
15 (© Gao Shanyue/Xinhua Press), 18 (©
Bettmann), 22 (© Jack Hollingsworth), 27
(© Blue Jean Images), 28 (© Christophe
Boisvieux), 36 (© Liu Liqun), 39 (© Steven
Vidler/Eurasia Press); Getty Images pp. 19
(Gamma-Keystone), 24 (RedChopsticks);
© Photoshot p. 41; Photoshot pp. 17 (©
Xinhua), 32 (© UPPA), 34, 35 (© Xinhua);
Shutterstock pp. 6 (© Roman Sigaev), 7 (©
Mikhail Nekrasov), 9 (© Stefano Tronci), 16
(© davidk), 23 (© Hung Chung Chih), 33 (©
Thomas Barrat), 43 top left (© Carlos Huang),
43 top right (© Hung Chung Chih), 43 bottom
left (© Ben Jeayes), 43 bottom right (© Jess
Yu), design features (© bluehand).

Cover photograph of a smiling Chinese boy
reproduced with permission of Alamy (©
Lonely Planet Images). Cover design feature of
a colourful textile reproduced with permission
of Shutterstock (© bluehand).

Every effort has been made to contact
copyright holders of any material reproduced
in this book. Any omissions will be rectified
in subsequent printings if notice is given to
the publisher.

# CONTENTS

Some words are shown in bold, **like this**. You can find out what they mean by looking in the glossary.

# INTRODUCING CHINESE CULTURE

What do you picture when you think of Chinese culture? Do you imagine dragons and temples? Or do you think of martial arts and chopsticks?

## What is culture?

**Culture** is the values, beliefs, and attitudes of a particular place. It is about how people live and worship, and about the music, art, and literature they produce. Chinese culture has developed over 4,000 years. This book explores different aspects of this ancient, colourful, and fascinating culture.

## Powerful rulers

For thousands of years, different parts of China were ruled by powerful emperors from different families called **dynasties**. Some of the most important dynasties were:

| | |
|---|---|
| Qin Dynasty | 221–206 BCE |
| Han Dynasty | 206 BCE –220 CE |
| Three Kingdoms | 220–280 CE |
| Southern and Northern Dynasties | 420–589 CE |
| Sui Dynasty | 581–618 CE |
| Tang Dynasty | 618–907 CE |
| Song Dynasty | 960–1279 CE |
| Ming Dynasty | 1368–1644 CE |
| Qing Dynasty | 1644–1911/12 CE |

Since 1912, China has been ruled by an elected government.

## Did you know?

There are over 1 billion people living in China: that is one-sixth of the world's total population. Over 90 per cent of people are Han Chinese, but there are many other **ethnic groups** including Zhuang, Manchu, Yi, Miao, Uighur, Jinuo, and Dong.

# ORNAMENT

Art and decoration are central to Chinese culture, from elaborate palaces and gardens, to fine silk painting, paper cutting, and beautiful writing. Many of the grandest buildings and monuments in China were designed around ideas of power, **superstition**, and **harmony** in nature.

*Feng shui* is a way of creating harmony between buildings and nature to improve quality of life. The Imperial Summer Palace (Qing Dynasty) and the Tiantan Temple (Ming Dynasty) were carefully built to follow the rules of *feng shui* by including ponds, wells, and even rivers.

## Forbidden City

Beijing's Forbidden City was built during the Ming Dynasty from 1406 to 1420. For over 500 years, the city was "forbidden" because ordinary people were not allowed to enter. Today, this vast complex of over 900 buildings and gardens is one of China's most important tourist attractions.

Today, the Forbidden City is popular with tourists.

## Did you know?

Chinese people believe that evil things travel in straight lines, so roofs are often curved to prevent evil from entering buildings. Little statues called door gods are hung on doorways to ward off evil.

### *Changcheng* – the Great Wall

Emperor Qin Shi Huangdi (259–210 BCE) of the Qin Dynasty ordered a wall to be built to protect his empire from invaders. This wall was extended over many centuries by different rulers. It became the Great Wall of China, the best-preserved section of which is 8,850 kilometres (5,500 miles) long.

The Great Wall of China is one of the most amazing structures on Earth.

## Porcelain

Craftspeople in China have been making and selling porcelain, a strong and beautiful type of pottery, since the 7th century CE. During the Ming Dynasty (1368 to 1644), different techniques for making porcelain were developed along with new **enamels**, which made the colours brighter. Natural scenes, dragons, and **legends** were hand-painted. Today, Ming vases are very valuable.

## Painting pictures

For hundreds of years, Chinese artists have painted nature, particularly birds, flowers, or blossoms. Many paintings included writing, too. In 2011, a modern painting by Qi Baishi was sold for more than £40 million.

China is famous for its silk and silk painting. Using quick brushstrokes, coloured inks are used to paint words and pictures on kites, fans, and screens.

These hand-painted porcelain vases are nearly 400 years old.

### Ai Weiwei (born 1957)

Ai Weiwei is a Chinese artist, photographer, and designer. His artwork has been displayed in galleries all around the world, including the Tate Modern in London. There, visitors walked across his *Sunflower Seeds* installation, which was made up of 100 million porcelain seeds.

## Did you know?

A Chinese legend says that Empress Leizu was the first person to discover silk more than 5,000 years ago. The story goes that she was sitting under a mulberry tree in her palace garden when a silk moth cocoon dropped into her cup of tea. As she pulled the cocoon out, it unravelled into a single thread of pure silk. After this discovery, the Chinese started to make silk and sold it across the world.

Artists use brushes to write and paint on silk.

## Writing and literature

Writing and paper are central to Chinese culture. Paper was invented in China in about 105 CE during the Han Dynasty. Bamboo stems or wood from the paper mulberry tree were soaked and boiled with lime. The pulp was then pressed flat and dried to make paper. Pi Sheng invented a printing press in the early 11th century, and books started to be printed.

## What is calligraphy?

**Calligraphy** is beautiful, decorative handwriting. The Chinese word for it is *shufa* and it is considered a great art. Children as young as five can go to calligraphy classes at weekends. In 2009, an 11th century scroll by Huang Tingjian was sold for over £40 million.

> ### Did you know?
> Chinese writing is made up of over 47,000 different characters but some of these are rarely used. Most people use 3,000 to 4,000 in their daily life.

Calligraphers practise for many years to perfect the art of writing with a brush.

## Books and ideas

At various times in history, books have been banned in China as the rulers believed the ideas in them were anti-government and dangerous. Today, there is greater freedom of reading but there is still some **censorship**.

### Wang Xizhi (303–361 CE)

Wang Xizhi was a calligrapher and is still regarded as the finest ever. The Emperor Taizong admired his works so much that he is supposed to have some of Wang's work buried with him.

## Clothes and fashion

Today, lots of Chinese people wear clothes from the United States and Europe, such as jeans and suits. In the countryside, handmade cotton tunic suits, known as Mao suits, are still worn. This style of suit was introduced around 1950 as a form of national dress. (See page 28 for more information on regional clothes.)

In ancient China, emperors and **officials** wore long silk **embroidered** gowns called "dragon robes". Court officials also wore badges to show their rank. For special occasions today, women might wear a dark robe called a *xuanduan* and men might wear a silk-embroidered *tangzhuang* jacket.

The silk cheongsam or *qipao* dress is still popular today.

## Ma Ke (born 1971)

Ma Ke is a Chinese fashion designer with her own fashion house called Wu Yong. She has shown her designs at shows around the world. She is inspired by traditional Chinese weaving and design. She also thinks it is important to protect the environment, so she uses recycled materials in her clothes.

## Jewellery

Chinese artists have been making silver, gold, and **jade** jewellery for over 4,000 years. In ancient China, men and women wore jewellery to show their **nobility** and wealth. Jewellery was put in the graves of important people. Then and now, the designs are influenced by **Buddhist symbols**. Jade was used for rings, headdresses, earrings, and combs.

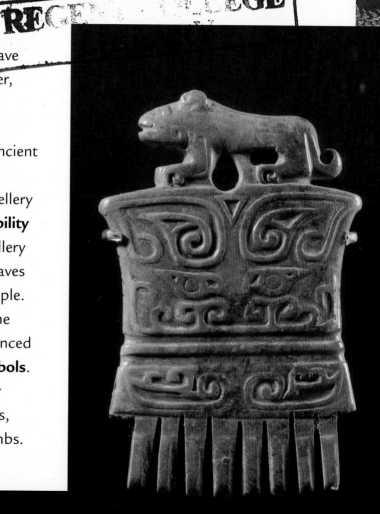

This jade comb dates from the 800s BCE.

# CUSTOMS, ACTIVITIES, AND COMMUNISM

Chinese people take part in many sports and activities that are good for physical strength as well as mental and spiritual health. Some sports invented in China have spread overseas and are now practised by millions worldwide.

## Martial arts

Martial arts are an ancient system of fighting, self-defence, and honour. Many Asian countries have their own styles of martial art and these are sometimes linked to religions, such as Buddhism. *Wushu* means "military skill" and is the general word for Chinese martial arts, such as *taijiquan* (shadow boxing). Historically, Chinese martial arts schools were quite secretive. This was to ensure national security and not give any information to China's enemies.

## YOUNG PEOPLE

There are many martial arts schools in northern China. Because martial arts are a way of life as well as a form of self-defence, these schools are often based in temples and are run by monks. Students have lessons in **philosophy**, health, and **meditation** as well as martial arts.

## Fighting with honour

Martial arts students are taught a code of ethics (to do with right and wrong). It means acting honourably and respecting their opponents. To practise, students fight each other. They also practise *qigong*, which is a way of breathing in time with your movements for maximum control.

### Jet Li (born 1963)

Jet Li is a Chinese actor and former champion martial artist. He has made many martial arts and action films in both China and the United States, including *Shaolin Temple* (1982), *Once Upon A Time in China* (1991), *Hero* (2002), and *The Expendables* (2010).

## Sports and games

Chinese people enjoy a mixture of traditional and modern games and activities. Board games such as chess, *majiang* (also known as *mahjong*), and *weiqi* were invented in China. *Weiqi* is believed to be over 2,000 years old. Two players use white and black stones to gain territory on a grid. In public parks throughout China, people meet to play these games. Chess and *majiang* are now played all over the world.

Chinese people today enjoy western sports such as horse racing, skateboarding, golf, and swimming. At the 2008 Olympic Games in Beijing, Chinese athletes won 100 medals. In 2011, Li Na became the first Chinese tennis player to win a **Grand Slam** when she won the French Open tournament.

In *majiang*, four players use 144 tiles with different Chinese characters and symbols on them.

## Yao Ming (born 1980)

Yao Ming is 2.29 metres (7 feet 6 inches) tall! Before he retired, Yao played basketball for the Houston Rockets in the NBA in the United States. He was the highest paid Chinese athlete in the world.

## Dancing and dragon boats

Many older people in China enjoy ballroom dancing classes. These often take place in parks. Younger people prefer dragon boat racing, which involves paddling to a drumbeat. Every year since 1976, an international dragon boat competition has been held in Hong Kong harbour.

Dragon boats have been raced in China for over 2,000 years.

## Politics and culture

China's government is made up of just one party, the Chinese **Communist** Party. The party has very strong ideas about how the country should be organized and how people should live. This has had a dramatic effect on Chinese culture.

Mao Zedong (1893–1976) was the first communist leader of China. He ruled from 1949 until his death. Some of his ideas helped to transform China into the superpower it is today. However, this was at the expense of human rights. Anyone who disagreed with his ideas was imprisoned or killed. Mao's ideas to improve the farming industry resulted in millions starving.

One of Mao's most disastrous ideas was the Cultural Revolution. From 1966 to 1976, Mao tried to reshape Chinese culture by forcing people to think as he wanted them to. Some ancient temples and **monasteries** were destroyed. Many books were burned and banned. Writers, artists, and musicians were killed or sent away for thinking differently from Mao.

This is Mao Zedong, pictured in 1966.

## New beginnings

Since the end of the Cultural Revolution in the late 1970s, traditional Chinese culture has started to thrive again. Today, Chinese artists receive government support for their work and Chinese people enjoy greater cultural freedom to express their thoughts and beliefs.

## Did you know?

Mao was a philosopher and poet, as well as the leader of his country. In 1966, *The Little Red Book*, a collection of his thoughts and speeches, was published. People were expected to read this book and follow his teachings. This picture from 1971 shows young people reciting passages from the *The Little Red Book*.

# BELIEFS AND FESTIVALS

Officially, there is no religion in China. However, **Daoism**, Buddhism, **Confucianism**, Islam, and Christianity are widely followed. Daoism was founded around 600 BCE by Laozi. *Dao* means "the way" and, like Buddhism, it teaches people how to live in harmony with nature and other people.

This Daoist temple in Beijing is decorated with special knots that are believed to be lucky.

## Buddhism

Around 200 CE, near the end of the Han Dynasty, Chinese people began to be influenced by a new religion from India called Buddhism. Buddhists believe that they can achieve a state of spiritual happiness known as nirvana through meditation.

Chinese Buddhist temples have towers in them called pagodas. Pagodas are used to store sacred objects, religious books, and treasures. Many pagodas have curved roofs, and Buddhist imagery and symbols carved into them.

## Confucius (551–479 BCE)

The philosopher Confucius is one of China's most celebrated thinkers. His teachings said that strong family ties were as important as personal responsibility and fairness. These values still influence Chinese culture today. One of his most famous sayings is "What you do not wish for yourself, do not do to others."

## *Yin* and *yang*

Chinese philosophy states that all living things are a mixture of *yin* and *yang*. *Yin* and *yang* are opposites but they rely on each other and are interconnected. Chinese people believe this creates balance and harmony.

*Yin* (the black section in the symbol on the right) represents Earth, femaleness, darkness, and passivity. *Yang* (the white section in the symbol) represents heaven, maleness, lightness, and activity.

## Did you know?

Chinese Buddhism has four sacred mountains: Wutai Shan, Emei Shan, Jiuhua Shan, and Putuo Shan. Pilgrims go to the mountains to pray at the temples there.

## Rituals and signs

From ancient times, Chinese people have been influenced by religion and superstition. For example, the Chinese believe that a house should never be cleaned on New Year's Day for fear that all the new good fortune will be swept away. It is also considered a lucky sign to see red-coloured birds on 1 January.

In Chinese culture, the luckiest number is 8. It sounds like the Chinese word for fortune. The number four is unlucky as it sounds like the word for death. Some high-rise buildings do not have a named fourth floor for this reason.

In temples, people consult bamboo sticks called *qian* for advice about problems in their lives.

## Animal calendar

A calendar of twelve animal signs was a way of naming the years in ancient China, and is still used today. For example, babies born in 2012 are born in the Year of the Dragon. See which animal represents you in the chart on the next page.

| | |
|---|---|
| Year of the Dragon | 2000/2012 |
| Year of the Snake | 2001/2013 |
| Year of the Horse | 2002/2014 |
| Year of the Goat | 2003/2015 |
| Year of the Monkey | 2004/2016 |
| Year of the Rooster | 2005/2017 |
| Year of the Dog | 2006/2018 |
| Year of the Pig | 2007/2019 |
| Year of the Rat | 2008/2020 |
| Year of the Ox | 2009/2021 |
| Year of the Tiger | 2010/2022 |
| Year of the Rabbit | 2011/2023 |

## Funeral customs

When people die, family members burn special paper houses and money for the dead. In ancient times, people celebrated their ancestors with picnics, music, and kite flying.

## Emperor Qin Shi Huangdi (259-210 BCE)

Emperor Qin Shi Huangdi wanted protection in the afterlife. A life-sized pottery army was buried with him. His tomb has not been opened yet but legend says that it is booby-trapped with armed crossbows and a river of poisonous mercury.

## Holidays and festivals

Chinese people celebrate many different festivals all over the country. The most important national ones are: Chinese New Year in January or February; International Labour Day, which is the first week of May; and National Day, which is celebrated during the first week of October.

## YOUNG PEOPLE

At New Year, relatives put money or sweets into envelopes called *hongbao* and put them under children's pillows. The amount of money usually ends in an even number as Chinese people believe this will bring good luck. *Hongbao* envelopes are red to represent good luck and ward off evil spirits.

At the end of the Spring Festival, towns and cities across China celebrate *Yuanxiaojie*, the Lantern Festival. Temples, parks, businesses, and homes are decorated with colourful lanterns made of paper and glass. Dragon and lion dances are performed in the streets.

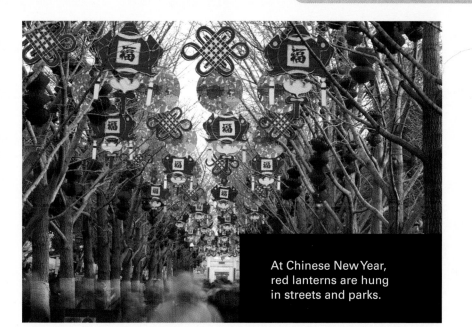

At Chinese New Year, red lanterns are hung in streets and parks.

## Sky and sea

Every year in April, the skies above the city of Weifang are filled with the sight of thousands of colourful kites at its kite festival. Drums, gongs, and music accompany this international festival.

The Qintong Boat Festival has taken place since the days of the Ming Dynasty. Lake Xique is filled with boats. Dragon and lion dances are performed on the boats and thousands watch the spectacle.

# FAMILY AND SOCIETY

Family is central to Chinese society. In most families today, the father is still the main provider for the family. However, many women also work. Children are mostly free to choose the career they want and the partner they want. However, they still respect their elders and seek their advice.

Children typically live with their parents until marriage. Afterwards, most couples live in small flats in the cities.

In the countryside, families live in wooden houses with tin or thatched roofs and cook over open fires. In the past, arranged marriages were common amongst farmers and country people. Today there is more freedom and choice.

### One-child policy

According to Chinese law, most couples are only allowed one child. This is a way of controlling population growth and to protect the country's **natural resources**.

In the countryside, where there is a shortage of workers, families are allowed to have more than one child. Some ethnic minority families are also excepted from the one-child policy. Traditionally, baby boys are favoured but this is slowly changing with better opportunities for women in society.

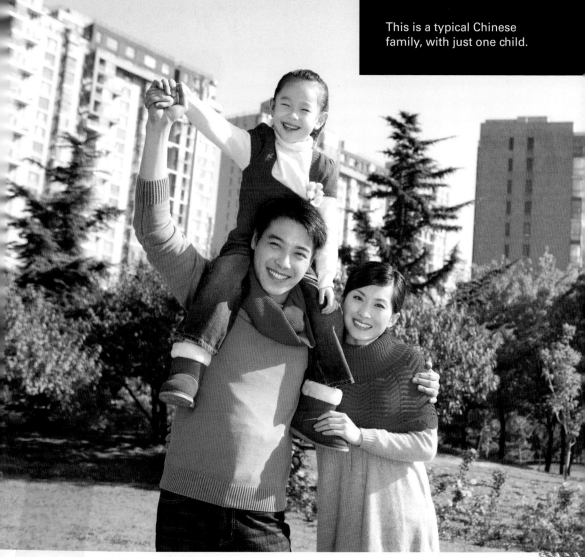

This is a typical Chinese family, with just one child.

## YOUNG PEOPLE

Today, many young people are leaving their country homes and travelling to the cities for work or to improve their education. This is changing country life in China as there are fewer people left to work the land and keep village communities going.

## YOUNG PEOPLE

Traditionally, marriages within the Yi people are arranged by parents. The bride's family demand engagement gifts of land or animals. Yi brides make wedding trousers for their grooms as a gift. The men then wear the trousers every day until the first child is born.

## Ethnic groups

There are over 50 different groups of people that make up China's vast population. Each group has its own particular way of life, language, and culture.

The Miao make up one of the largest ethnic groups in China, with around 9 million people. Miao are very skilled at making jewellery.

These Miao girls are wearing decorative silver jewellery. The girl on the right is playing a *lusheng* (see page 29).

Miao have their own traditional wind instrument, a reed mouth organ known as the *lusheng*, which is played at festivals.

Around 20,000 Jino people live mainly in Yunnan province. They worship the god *Amo Yaobai*, who they believe created the sky and the land. Their most important festival is the Iron Forging Festival. During this, Jino dance to the Sun Drum and hope for a good harvest.

There are over 2.5 million Dong people living in Guizhou and Hunan provinces. They are farmers and foresters. The women are known for their spinning and embroidery. Most of their clothing is blue, black, white, and purple.

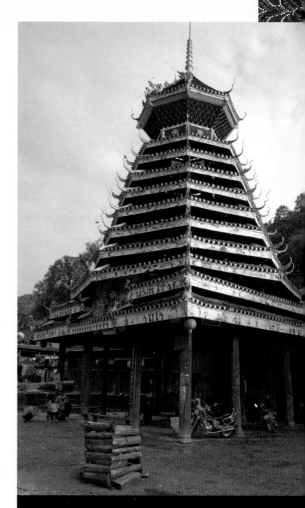

This is a Drum Tower, a traditional wooden structure built by the Dong people.

## Did you know?

The Dong people of southern China think ahead. When a child is born, they plant a group of pine trees. When the child becomes an adult at 18, the trees are cut down and used to build a house for the young person.

## Food and drink

People all over the world enjoy eating Chinese food, such as noodles, crispy duck, and **wontons**. In China, food is cooked in woks or bamboo basket steamers, and people eat out of bowls with chopsticks. Today, Chinese people are eating more meat and wheat like people in the West.

### Ching-He Huang (born 1978)

Ching-He Huang is a Chinese television chef and best-selling author based in London. Her cooking is influenced by traditional Chinese cooking but with a modern twist. Her television programmes try to make Chinese food simple and introduce unusual ingredients to the viewers.

## Festival foods

Moon cakes are eaten during the mid-autumn festival. These sweet pastry cakes have a salted egg yolk in the centre to symbolize the full moon. On the top of the cake are the Chinese characters for "long life" or "harmony" and a picture of the Moon. During the Duanwu festival of dragon boat racing, special rice dumplings called *zongzi* are eaten.

## Drinking tea

In China, drinking tea is not only part of people's daily lives, but is also connected with religions such as Daoism and Buddhism. In these faiths, drinking tea is an important part of developing yourself. Traditionally, tea drinkers were important people because drinking tea showed a good level of education.

Today, tourists visit traditional Chinese teahouses, such as this one in Shanghai. They can choose from hundreds of different teas.

## Health and medicine

Chinese people's way of life and medicine are focused on well-being. Traditional Chinese medicine is known as *zhong yi*, and is based on the *yin* and *yang* philosophy of balance and energy. It is believed that a person's *qi* (energy flow) is central to being healthy. *Qi* can be helped by eating and drinking certain foods and by practising acupuncture. Acupuncture is the practice of putting fine needles into the skin at certain points to encourage *qi* balance.

Acupuncture is now practised all around the world.

### Sun Simiao (581–682 CE)

Sun Simiao was a doctor during the Sui and Tang Dynasties. He is known as the God or King of Medicine. Two of his books, *Qianjin Yaofang* and *Qianjin Yifang*, are still read today. They include many recipes for medicines. He also wrote "Thirteen measures to keep healthy", which included rolling your eyes and shaking your head!

## Did you know?

Early in the morning, in town and city parks all over China, thousands of people gather to perform *taiji*. *Taiji* involves gentle, controlled movements and meditation. Chinese people believe that *taiji* puts them in a positive frame of mind to start the day.

## Herbal cures

Chinese medical knowledge is thousands of years old and today this knowledge is appreciated by people all over the world. Acupuncture, herbal cures, and *Tui Na* massage are used to treat many illnesses and complaints. Modern aspirin is a chemical version of willow bark, a plant the Chinese have been using for pain relief for centuries.

# PERFORMANCE

China has an ancient tradition of music and performance. Opera and dance are still very popular forms of entertainment.

## Painted faces

Chinese opera stories are tales of heroes, legends, and **mythical** creatures. Acrobats, jesters, martial artists, and storytellers combine to create a colourful show. Actors paint their faces with bright colours to symbolize their character. For example, the hero usually has a red face, which means courage and support. A blue face means the character is cruel, a white face means a wicked character, and jesters have white noses.

This actress is being made up to look like a ghost. She will be performing in a Chinese opera.

## Harmony through movement

Chinese dance has always been linked with religion and harmony. Many of the movements are linked to Daoism and Buddhism, and are concerned with *jin* (concentration), *qi*, and *shen* (spirit). Some dances are about praying to the gods, whilst others are about showing fighting techniques or celebrating nature.

The Dragon Dance is part of the New Year celebrations. Teams of up to 50 people carry the dragon on poles. Moving to music, the dance tells the story of the dragon and its power. The dance was invented thousands of years ago to entertain emperors.

### YOUNG PEOPLE

Today, growing numbers of young people in China and in Chinese communities around the world are learning traditional dances at special workshops. These dances include the Ribbon Dance, the Silk Fan Dance, the Sword Dance, and the Long Sleeve Dance.

In Chinese culture, dragons are believed to bring good luck.

## Film and television

Most homes in China have a television. There are dozens of channels but many programmes are made and broadcast by the government-run Chinese Central Television. News and programme content is very strictly controlled by the government. Chinese soap operas, such as *A Watchdog's Tale*, are popular but any criticism of the government is banned and foreign programmes and films are often censored.

This family is enjoying a soap opera on television.

### Lu Chuan (born 1971)

Lu Chuan is one of China's most famous film directors. His films *Kekexili: Mountain Patrol* (2004) and *City of Life and Death* (2009) have won prizes at film festivals around the world. His films are inspired by Chinese culture and history.

## Making films

Made mostly in Hong Kong, *wuxia* films are popular throughout China and Asia. Jackie Chan is the best-known actor in these films, which he also directs. Feng Xiaogang, Jiang Wen, and Zhang Yimou are successful Chinese film directors who have won prizes at home and abroad. Films such as *Hero* (2002) and *House of Flying Daggers* (2004) mix *wuxia* superheroes with magical powers, and love stories.

## YOUNG PEOPLE

The Chinese government has projects and grants to support new young film directors. Making films and videos is very popular in China and many young artists upload their work to the internet in the hope of reaching an international audience.

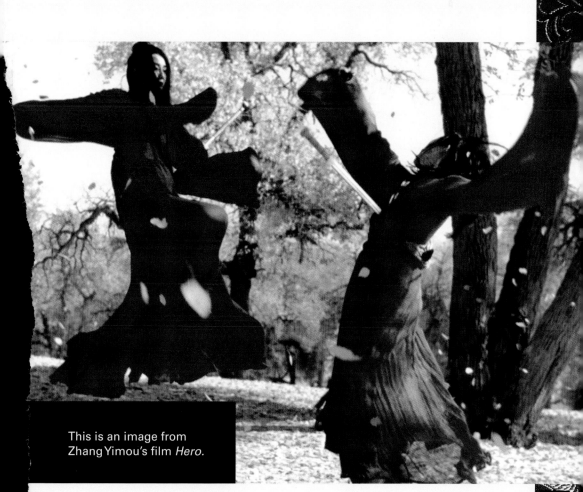

This is an image from Zhang Yimou's film *Hero.*

## Making music

According to Chinese mythology, Ling Lun was the founder of music. It is said that he made bamboo pipes which he tuned to the sounds of birdsong. Music has long been important in Chinese culture. The Imperial Music Bureau was established during the Qin Dynasty, over 2,000 years ago, and was responsible for all official music. Today, the Central Conservatory of Music in Beijing is the top music school in the country.

Chinese people today enjoy all sorts of music, from rock to traditional **folk** songs. Artists such as Tang Dynasty, Hei Bao, and Anita Mui are popular. The government does, however, censor some song words because it believes they are critical of the government.

### Cheng Maoyun (1900–1957)

Cheng Maoyun was a violinist and composer. In 1928, he wrote a tune called "The Three Principles of the People" for a competition. He won and the tune became the Chinese national anthem.

*Guo yue* means "national music" and it includes all music played at state events. It is played on traditional Chinese instruments and is meant to encourage national pride.

## Traditional instruments

There are many Chinese musical instruments, including the popular *erhu*, a type of violin. Most regions have special music schools where talented youngsters can study ancient or modern instruments.

## YOUNG PEOPLE

The Firebird Youth Orchestra of China is based in San Francisco, USA. The musicians range from 7 to 18 years old, and play only traditional Chinese instruments such as *sheng*, *yangqin*, and *ruan*.

These musicians are playing traditional Chinese stringed instruments and drums.

# CHINESE CULTURE IN THE 21ST CENTURY

China today is a country where old customs are increasingly giving way to modern life but where many traditions remain. Family remains important, as does faith, art, lifestyle, and tradition.

## Global impact

The spread of Chinese culture across the world is seen in many areas, from food to theatre, to medicine, to Chinatowns in major global cities. Today, Chinese athletes are making an impression on the world stage and Chinese musicians are gaining international fame. Chinese inventors have given the world fireworks, paper, and printing.

## Future impact

In this century, China is likely to become the most powerful country in the world. It has the world's fastest growing economy and a rapid rate of development in all areas of society. This will mean that more Chinese people will be able to afford to do more cultural activities and to travel.

In the last ten years, China has hosted the Olympics, developed its art and film industry, and started to revive its cultural traditions. It is a country that is aware of its cultural past and very firmly in control of its global future.

## YOUNG PEOPLE

Through technology and the internet, young people are learning more about other cultures around the world and other ways of doing things. The Chinese government censors online information and social networking sites but young people are starting to demand change.

Many cities all over the world have large Chinese communities. This colourful arch can be found in Liverpool's Chinatown.

# TIMELINE

# CULTURAL MAP

Lantern Festival

Forbidden City

N

HEILONGJIANG

JILIN

XINJIANG UYGUR

LIAONING

Disputed border

GANSU

NEI MONGOL

**Beijing**

HEBEI

NINGXIA SHANXI

SHANDONG

QINGHAI

SHAANXI

XIZANG

C H I N A

HENAN

JIANGSU

ANHUI

SICHUAN

HUBEI

CHONGQING

ZHEJIANG

GUIZHOU HUNAN

JIANGXI

YUNNAN

GUANGXI

FUJIAN

GUANGDONG

TAIWAN

Hong Kong

HAINAN

| 0 | 800 kilometres |
| 0 | 500 miles |

Terracotta Army

Dragon boat racing

# GLOSSARY

**Buddhism** religion based on the teaching of Buddha

**calligraphy** decorative handwriting

**censorship** process of officially preventing people from expressing ideas and opinions

**communist** someone belonging to a political system called communism

**Confucianism** system of belief based on the teachings of Confucius

**culture** customs, social organisation, and achievements of a particular nation, people, or group

**Daoism** religion based on simple living in harmony with nature

**dynasty** series of rulers from the same family

**embroidery** art of creating raised designs with thread

**enamel** paint-like coating put onto metal, glass, and ceramics

**ethnic group** group of people who share a common background, language, and culture

**folk** traditional form of music

**Grand Slam** in tennis, the Grand Slams are the four biggest tournaments in the world. They are the Australian Open, the French Open, the US Open, and Wimbledon.

**harmony**  balance between all elements

**jade**  hard stone, usually green, used for ornaments and jewellery

**legend**  old story that is passed down as history but is probably not true

**meditation**  clearing the mind and controlling the breathing

**monastery**  place where monks live

**mythical**  from stories and tales belonging to a particular people or culture

**natural resource**  material that occurs naturally

**nobility**  high social status

**official**  someone in charge of a government department

**philosophy**  system of beliefs guiding people in how to live well

**superstition**  belief that good or bad things will happen, but not based on fact

**symbol**  sign

**wonton**  type of dumpling

# FIND OUT MORE

## Books

*Ancient China (Cultural Atlas for Young People)*, Tony Allan (Facts on File Inc., 2007)

*China (A World of Food)*, Clare Hibbert (Franklin Watts, 2010)

*China (Countries in our World)*, Oliver James (Franklin Watts, 2009)

*China (Discover Countries)*, Susan Crean (Wayland, 2010)

*China (Welcome to My Country)*, Goh Sui Noi and Lim Bee Ling (Franklin Watts, 2010)

## Websites

www.fyco.org/new/orchestra_sections.html
Click on the pictures of each Chinese instrument to hear the sounds they make.

kids.nationalgeographic.com/kids/places/find/china/
Find out more about China's history, architecture, people, and culture.

https://www.cia.gov/library/publications/the-world-factbook/geos/ch.html
Find up-to-the-minute facts about China on this website.

## DVDs

*Great Wall of China* (2008)

*Lost in China* (National Geographic, 2011)

*Lost Treasures of the Ancient World: Ancient China* (2006)

## Places to visit

**British Museum, London**
www.britishmuseum.org
See ancient bronze and jade ornaments and household objects
in the China galleries of this amazing museum.

If you ever get the chance to go to China, these are some places
you could visit:

**Forbidden City, Beijing**
See how the emperors lived in the lap of luxury.

**Terracotta Army, Xi'an**
See the mighty warriors armed and waiting to defend the tomb
of the first Qin emperor.

**The Great Wall**
Look out for incoming raiders from this amazing structure.

**The Gardens of the Humble Administrator, Suzhou**
See how *yin* and *yang* and the ancient Chinese belief in *feng shui*
created this beautiful  garden.

## More topics to research

What topic did you like reading about most in this book? Did you
find out anything that you thought was particularly interesting?
Choose a topic that you liked, such as food, buildings, or religion,
and try to find out more about it. You could visit one of the places
mentioned above, have a look at one of the websites, or visit your
local library to do some research. You could also try some things
out – try making moon cakes, brush up on your calligraphy, or
enjoy a martial arts film.

# INDEX